MC PUFF

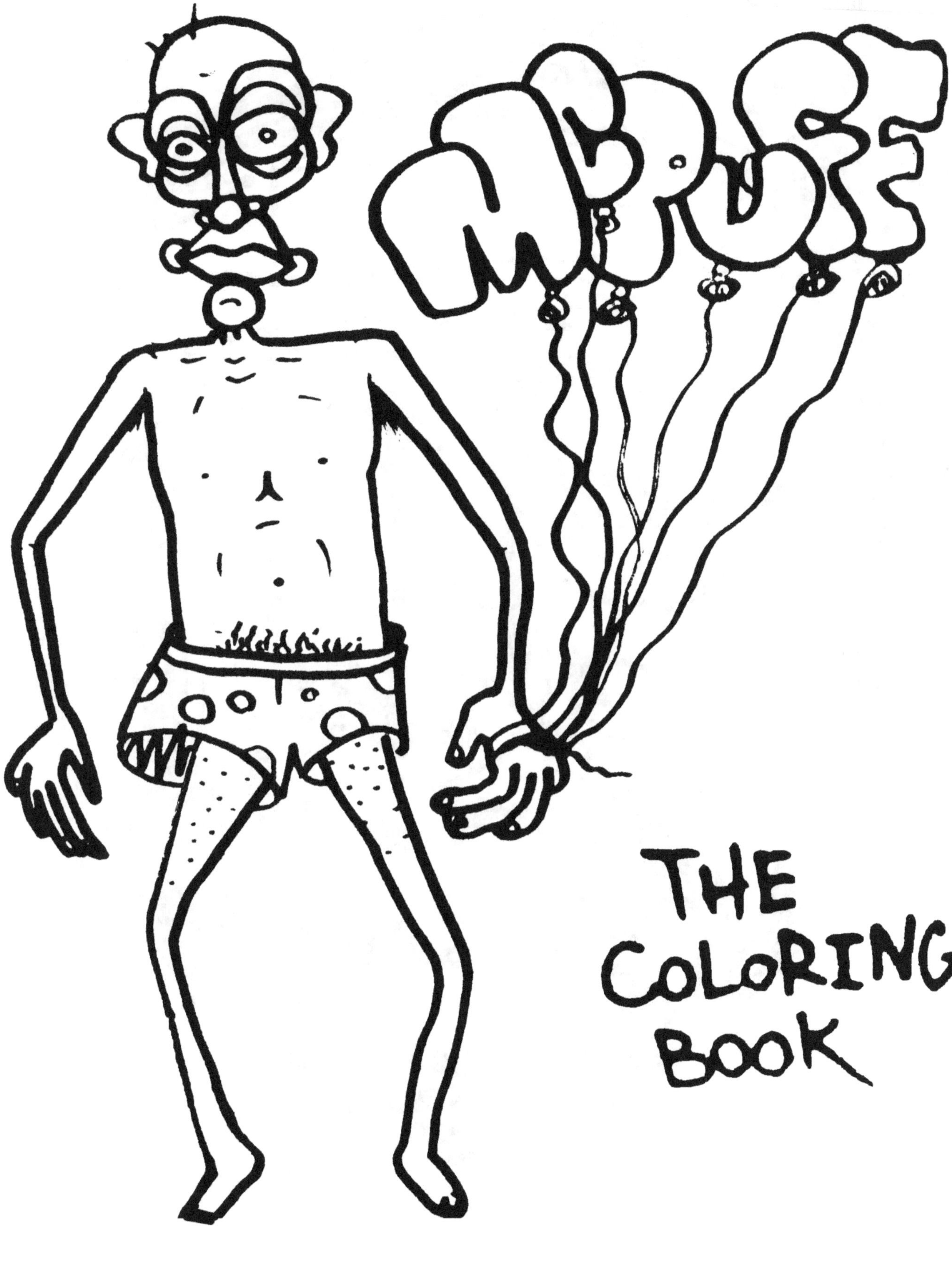

THE COLORING BOOK

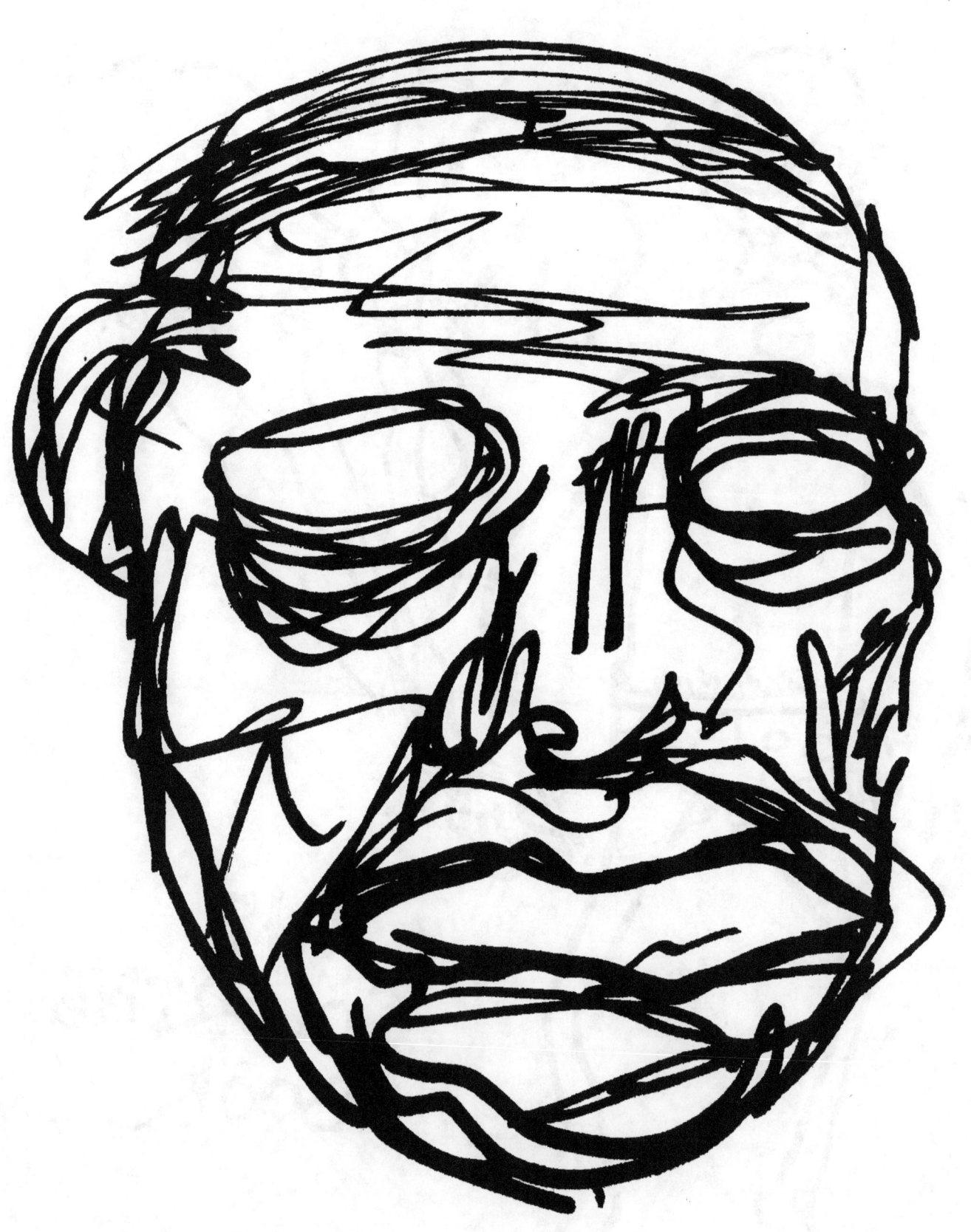

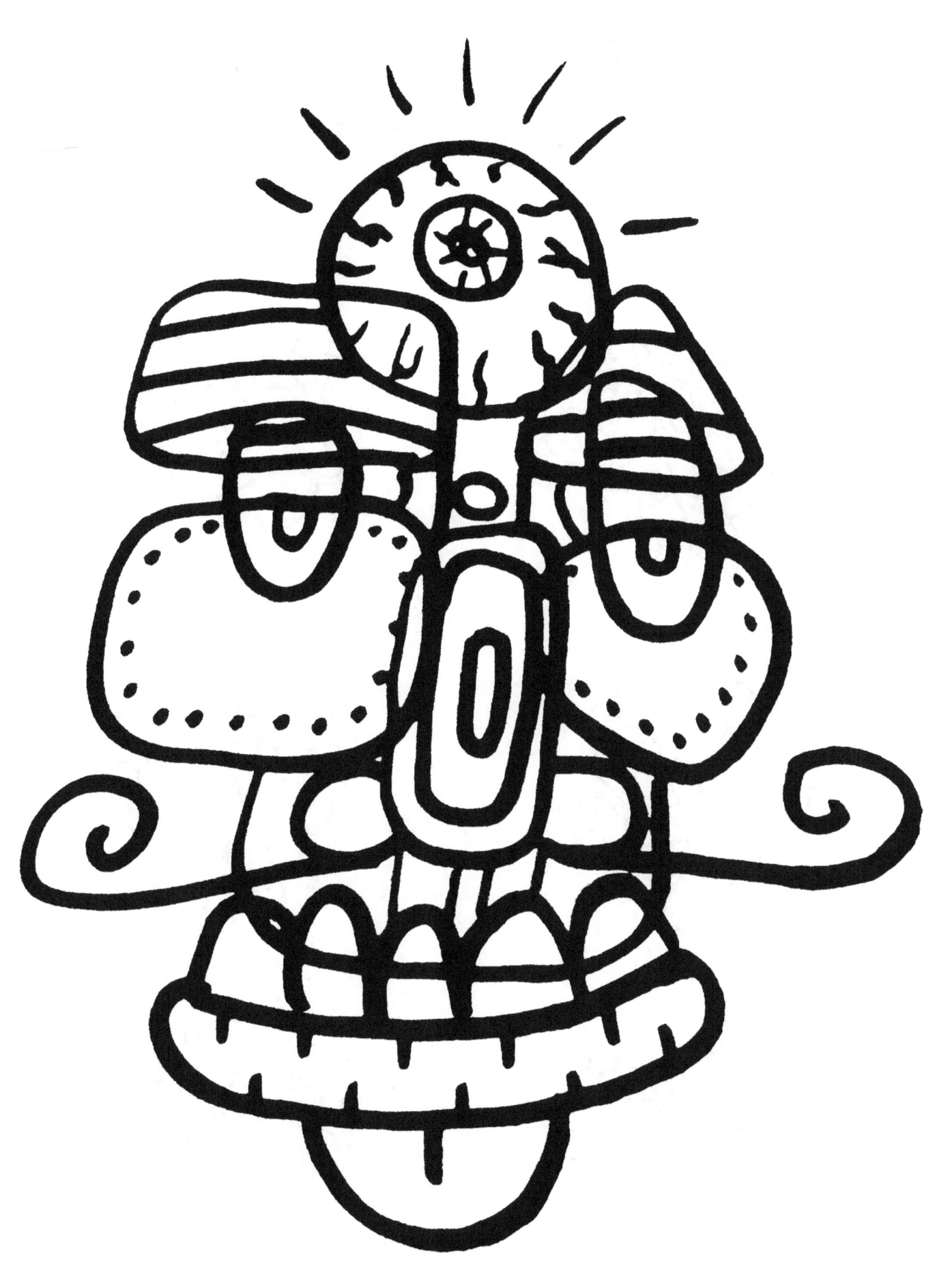

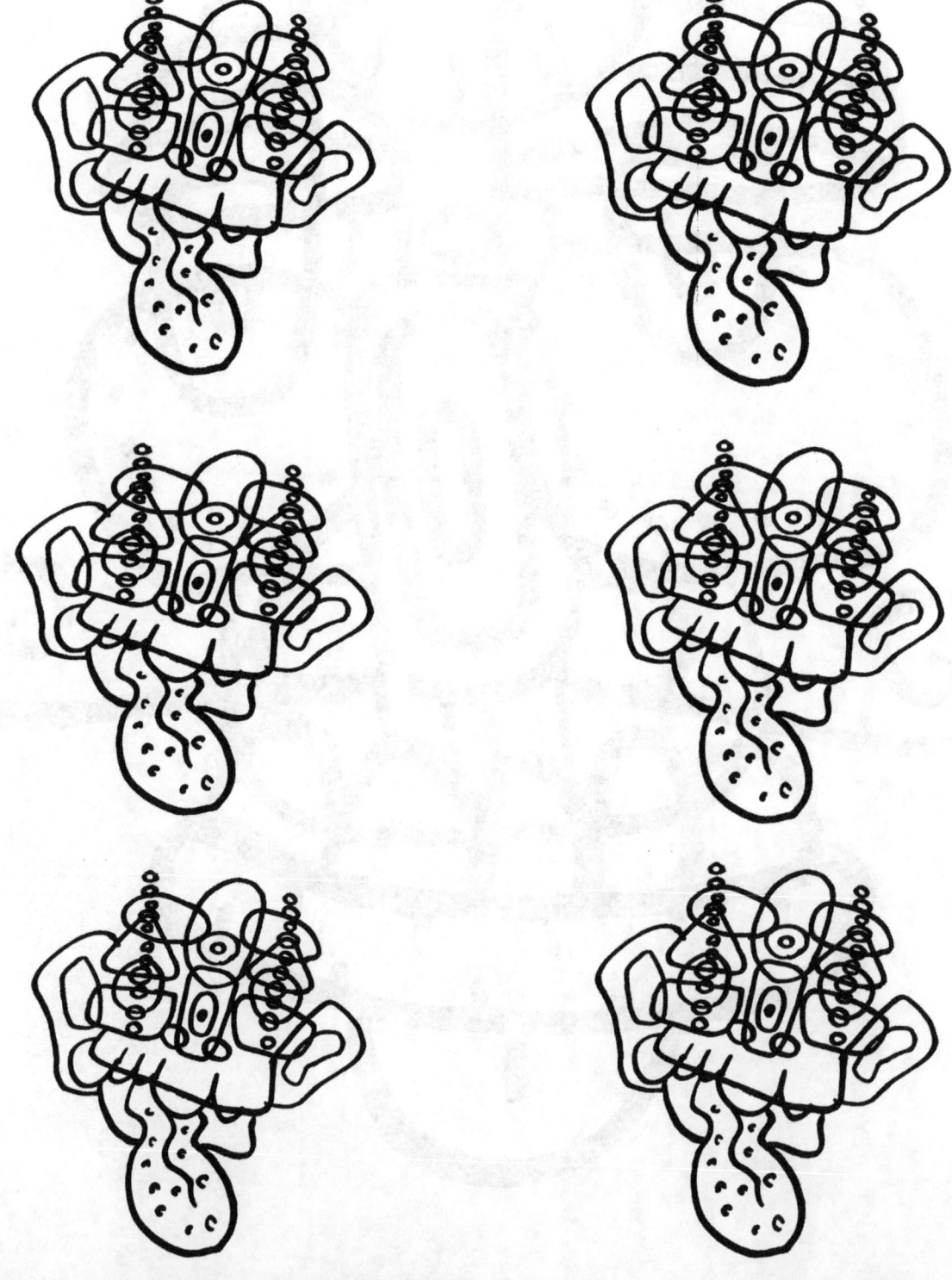

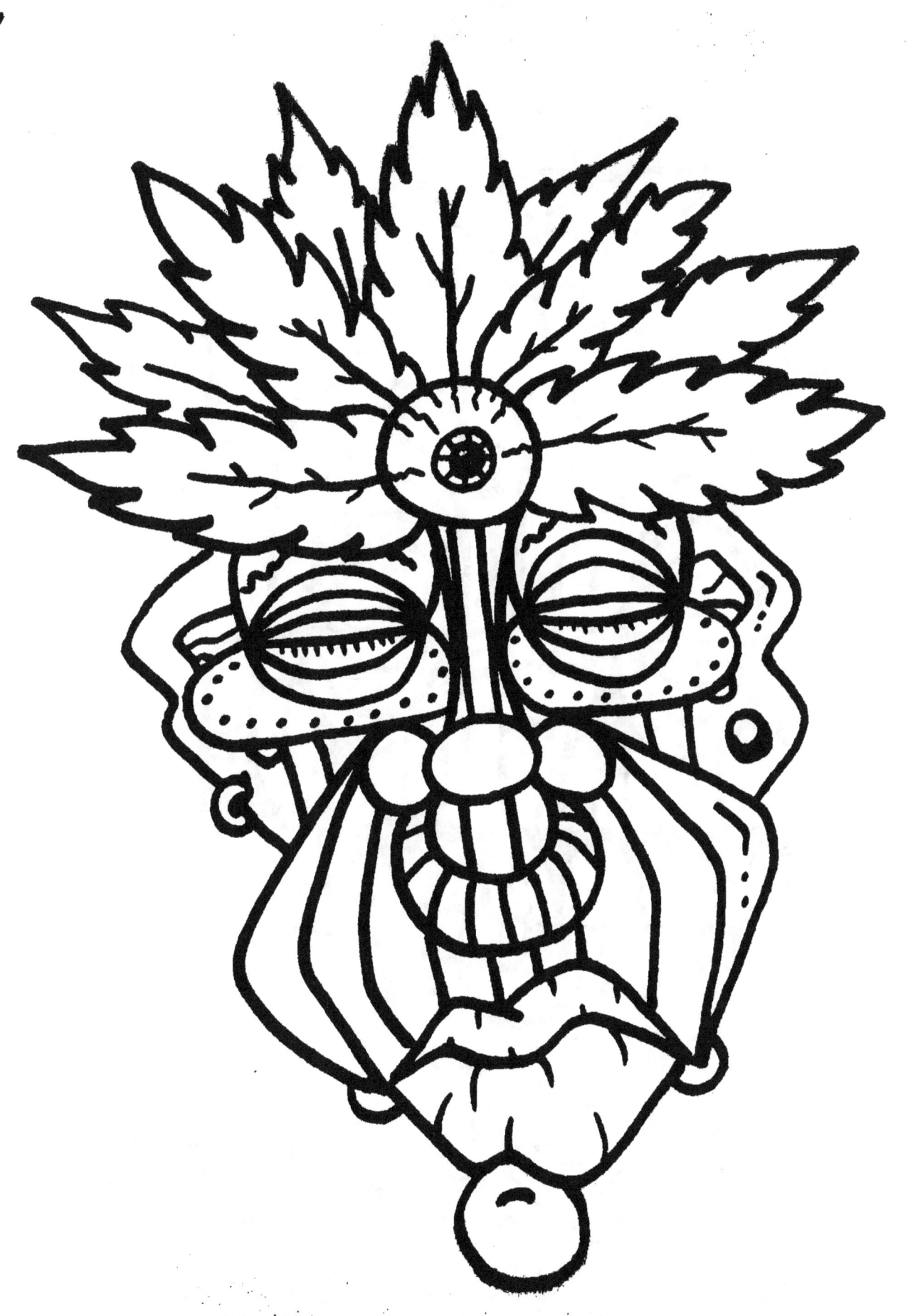

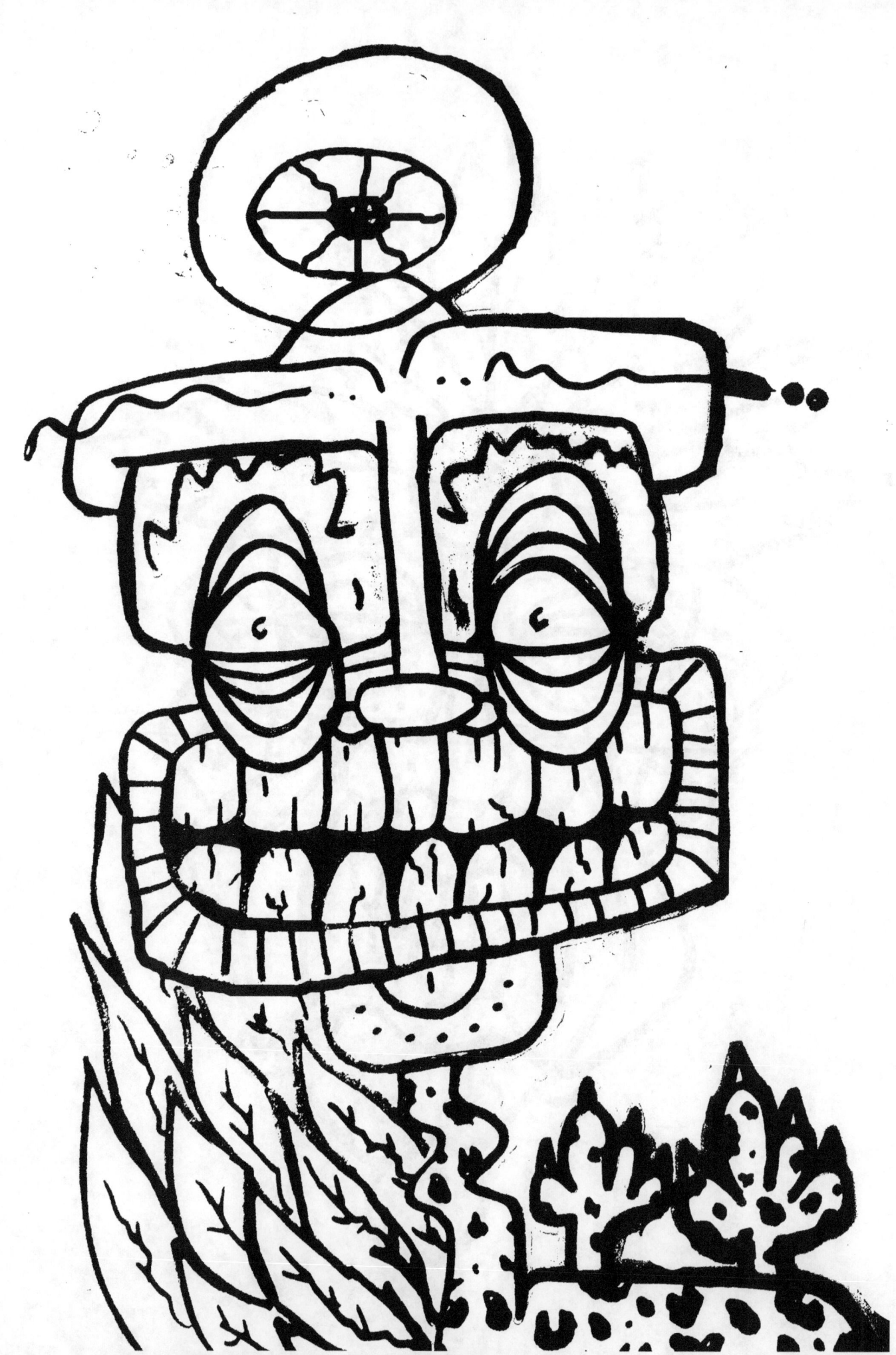

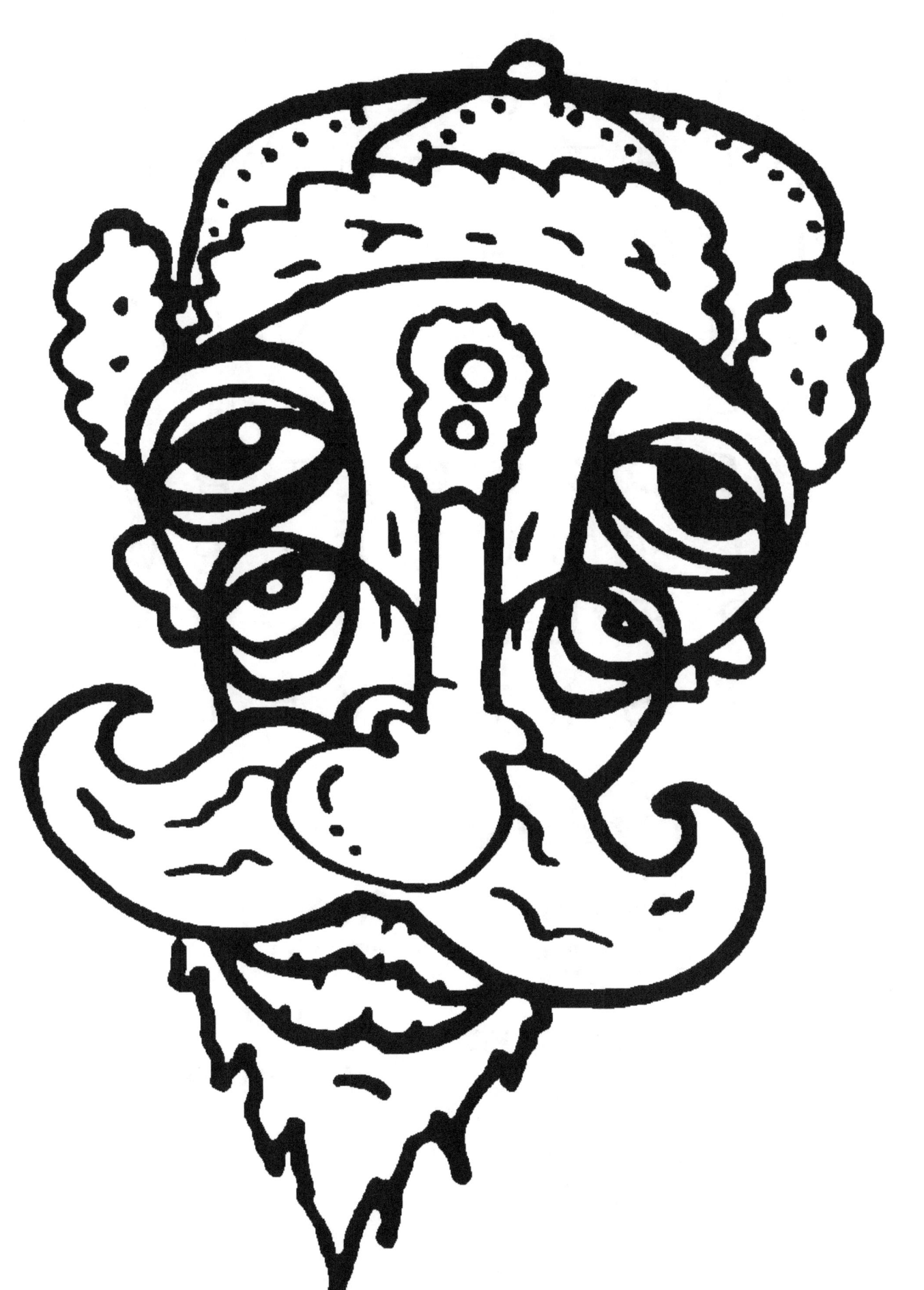

```
C T E Y E B A L L J
O K H T F F U P C M
L N D I A Z Y Y T Y
O N O L R R G O T N
R G I O A D N G H T
I E Q M L G E T B V
N L I N U L E Y B W
G D R E D E A Y E X
S T S N T V V B T L
```

Find these words:

Eyeball   Tongue

McPuff   Teeth

Third Eye   Balloon
                 Coloring
Alien

Pyramid

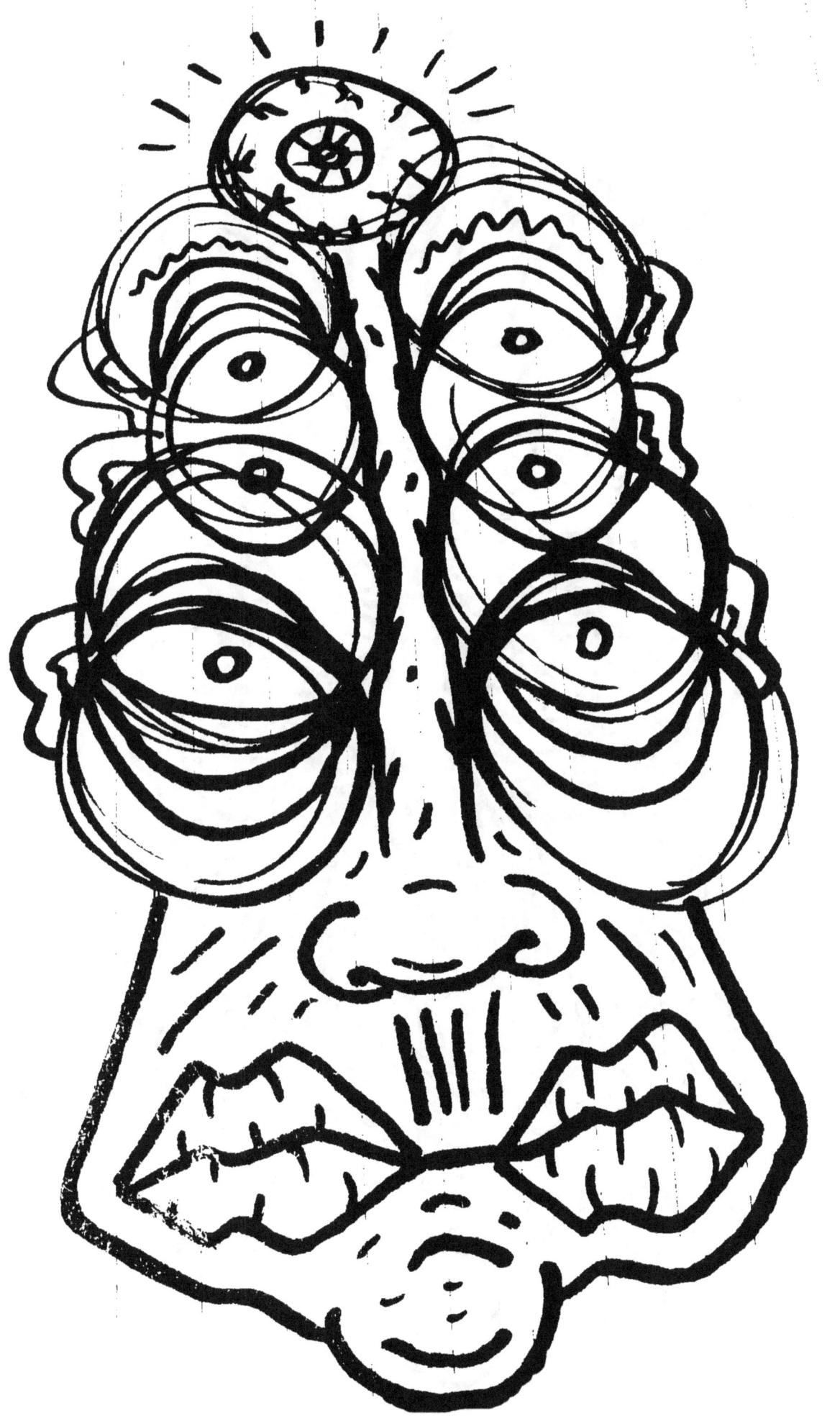

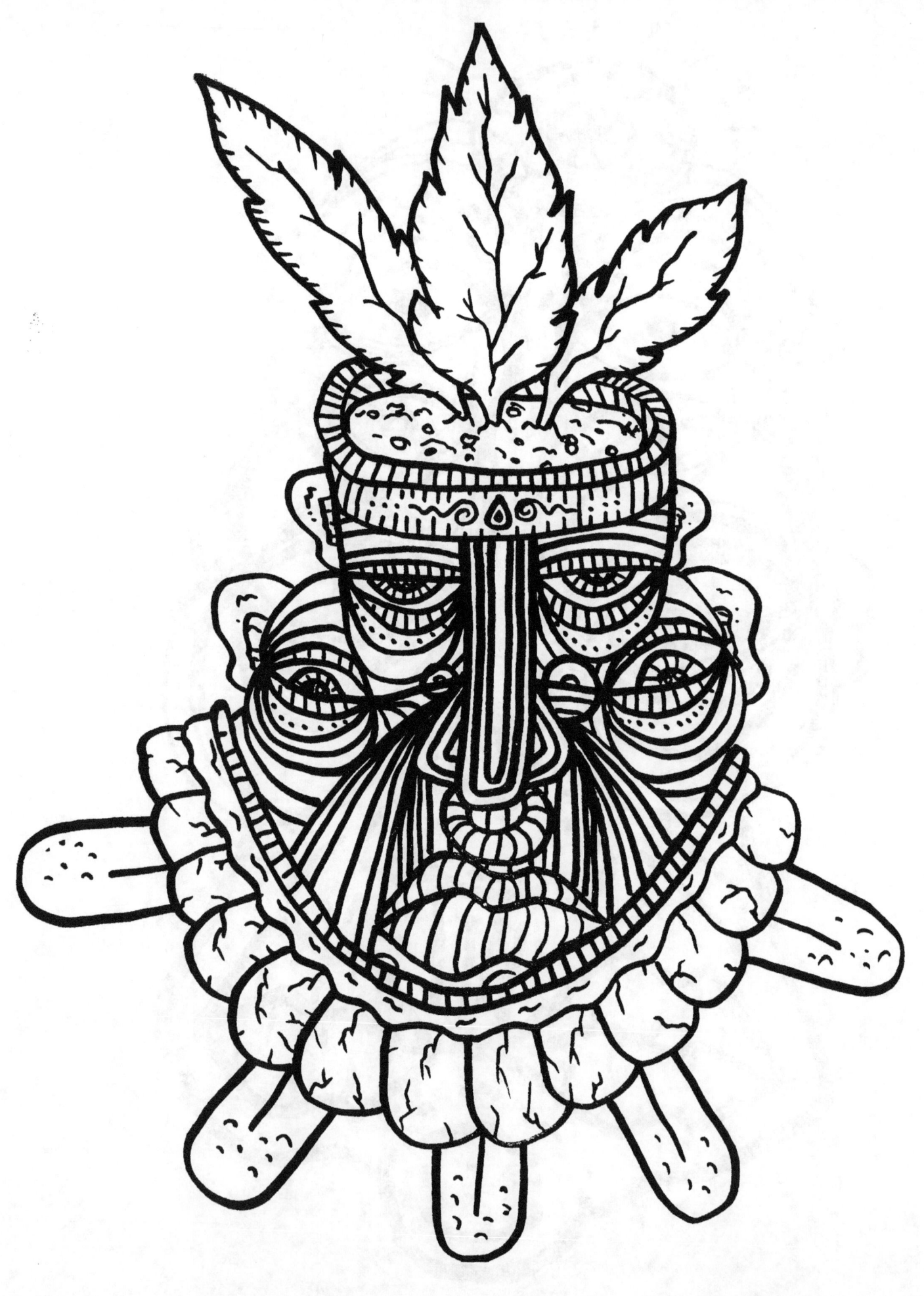

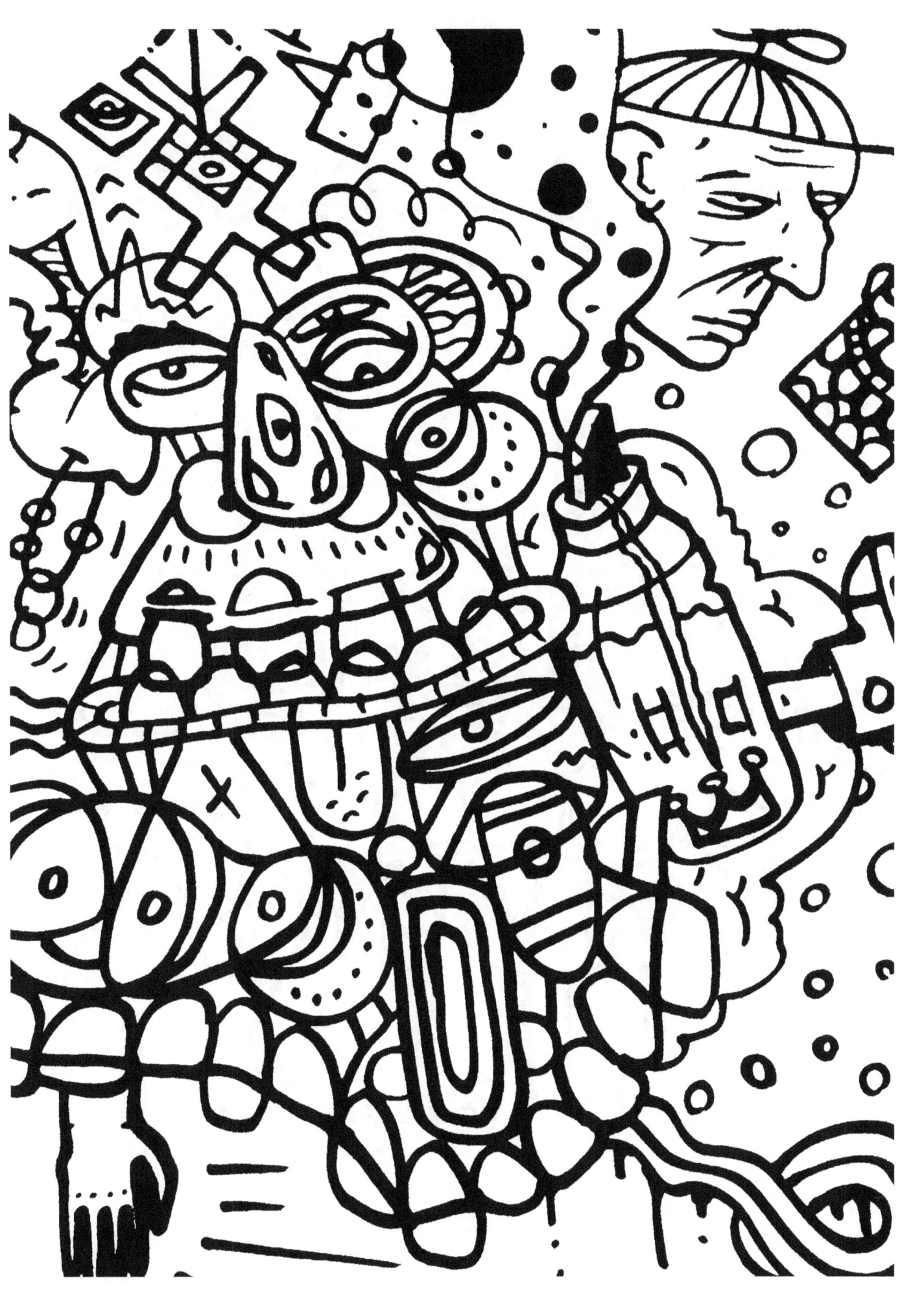

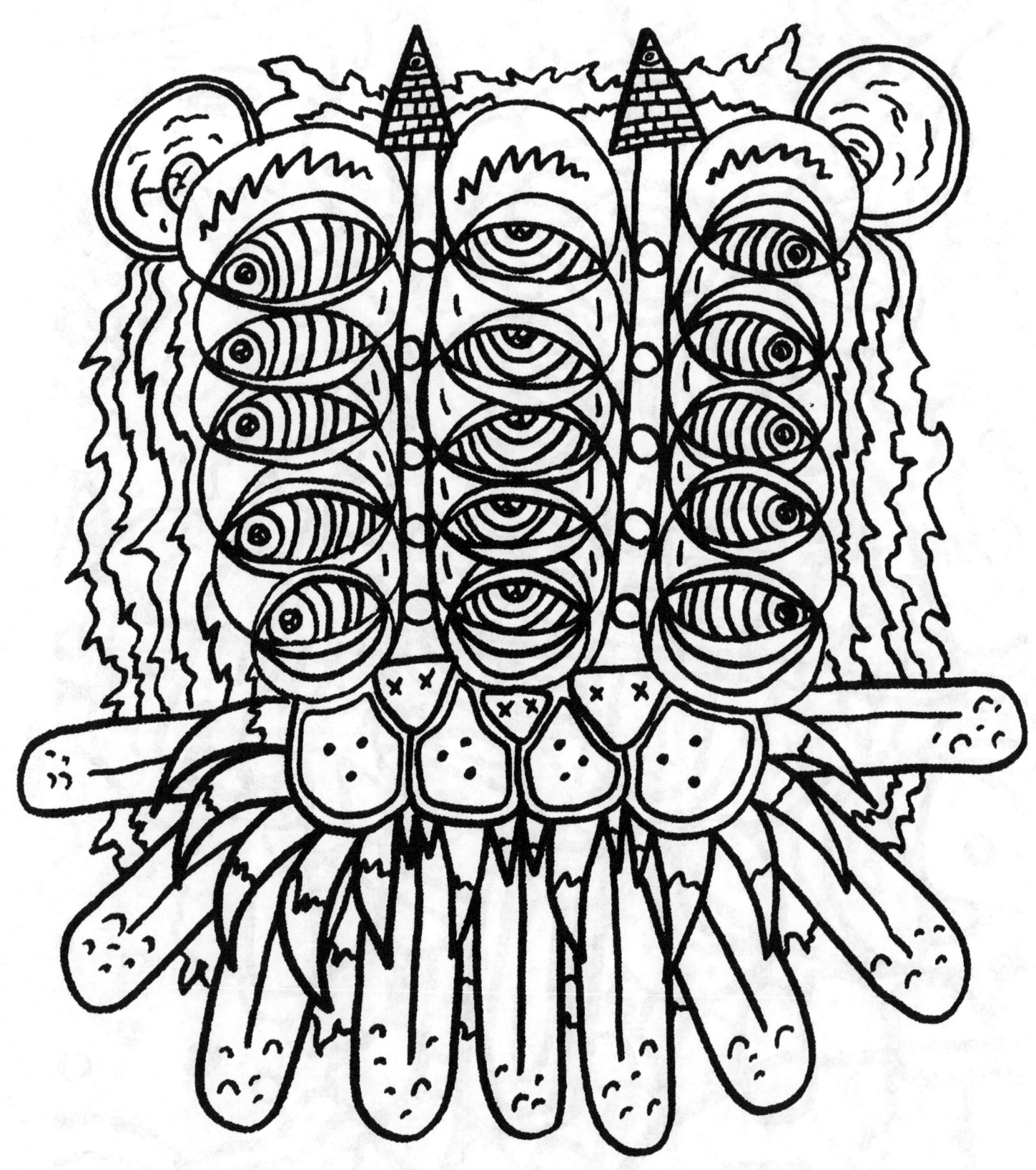

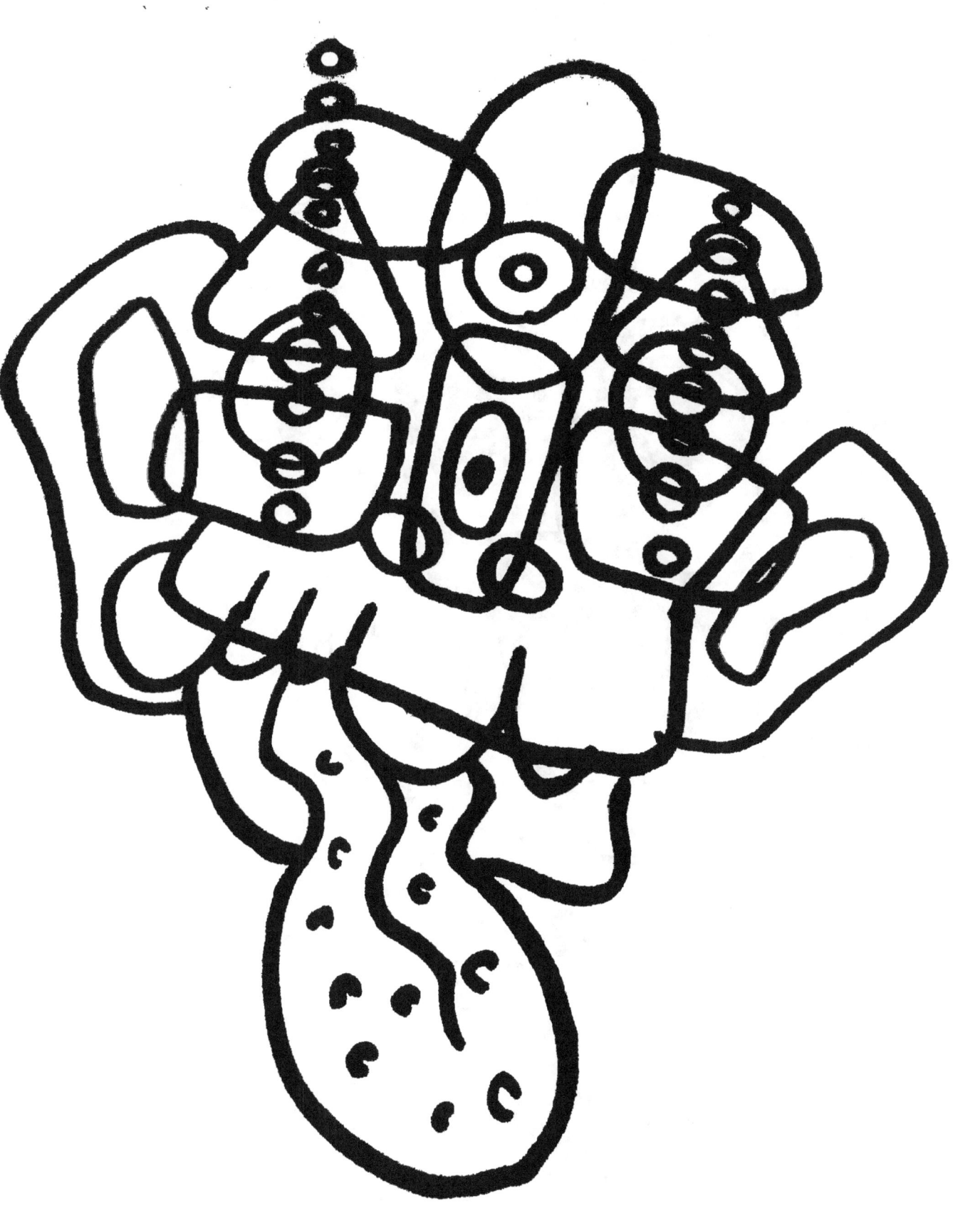

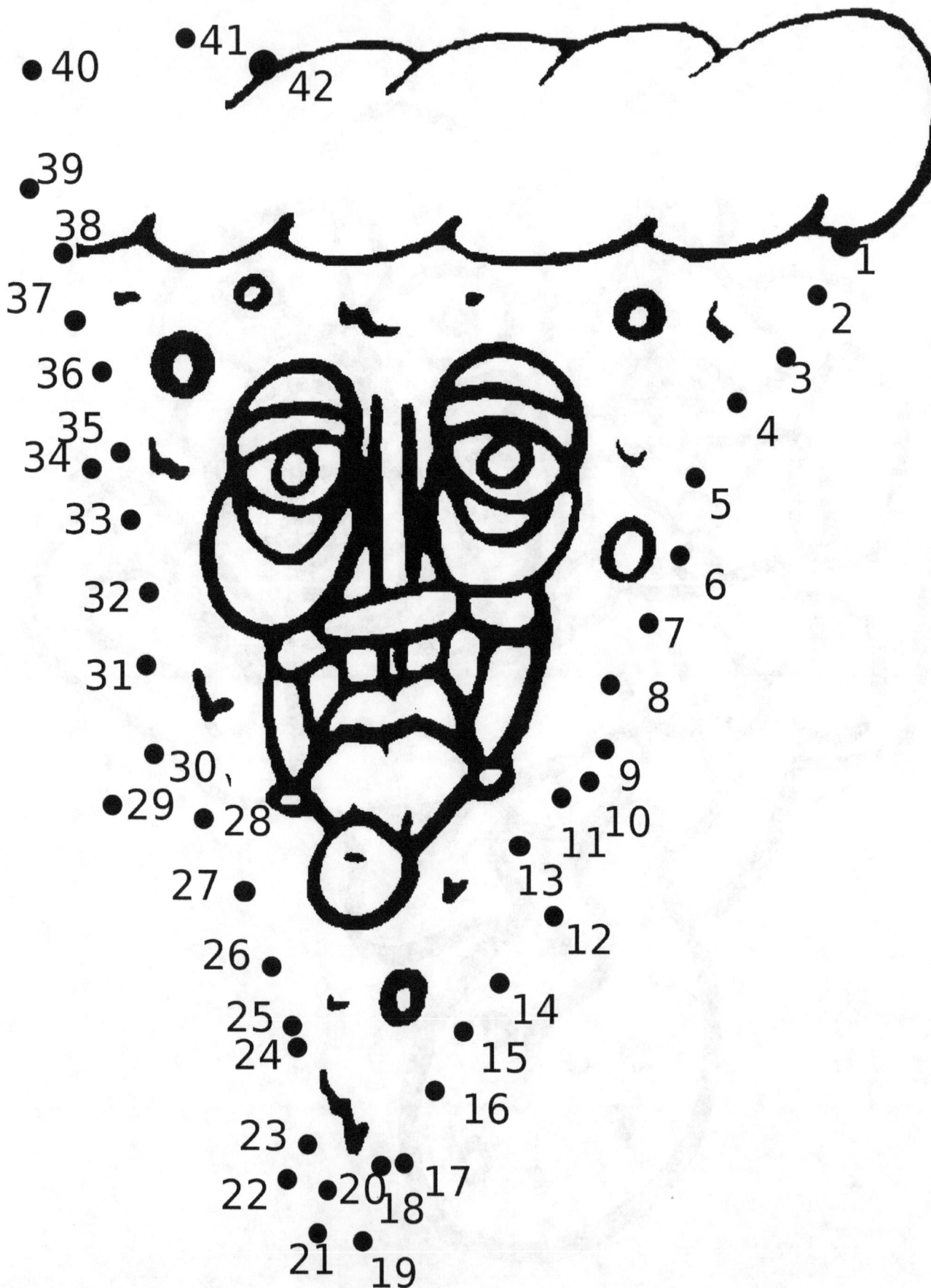

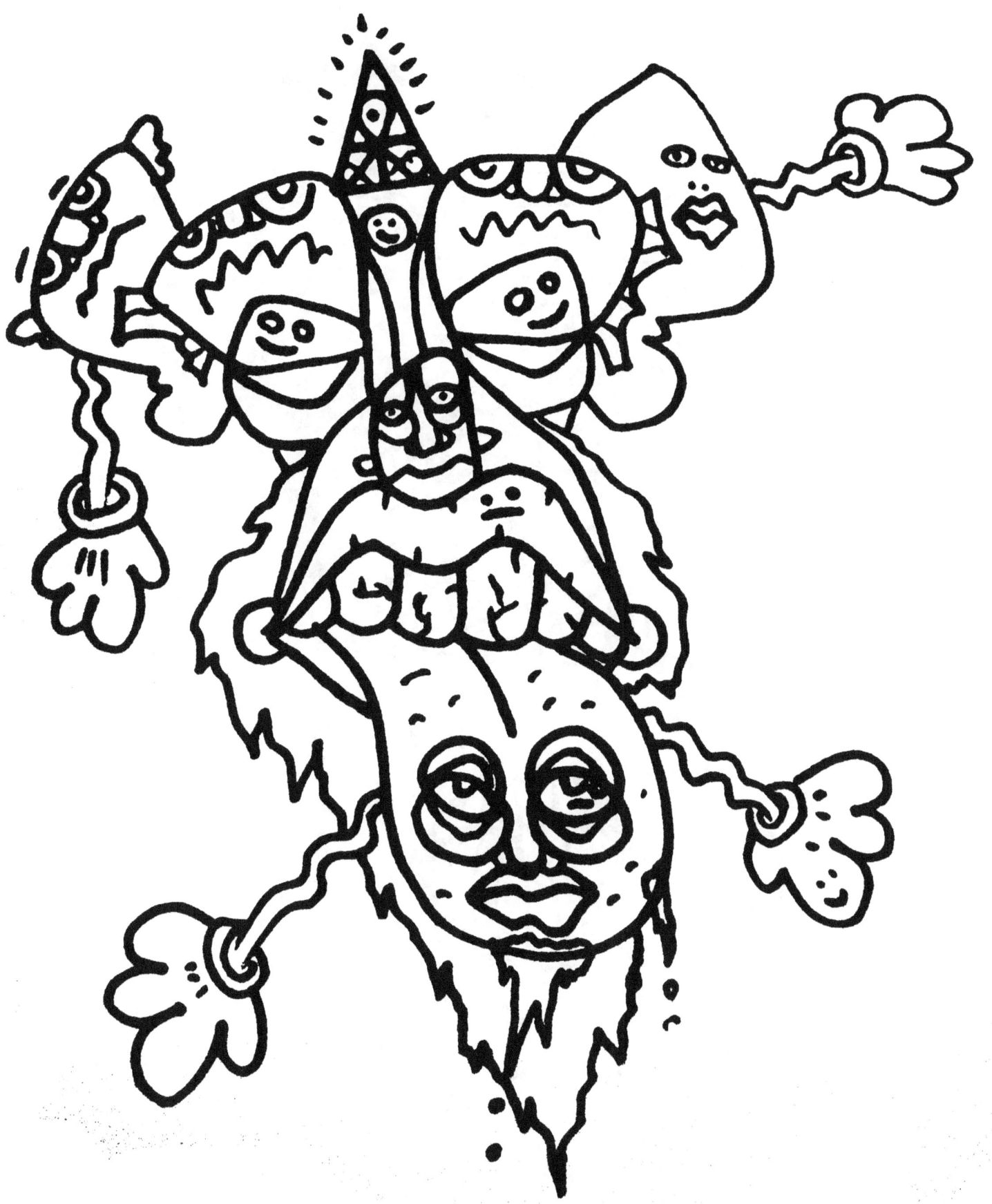

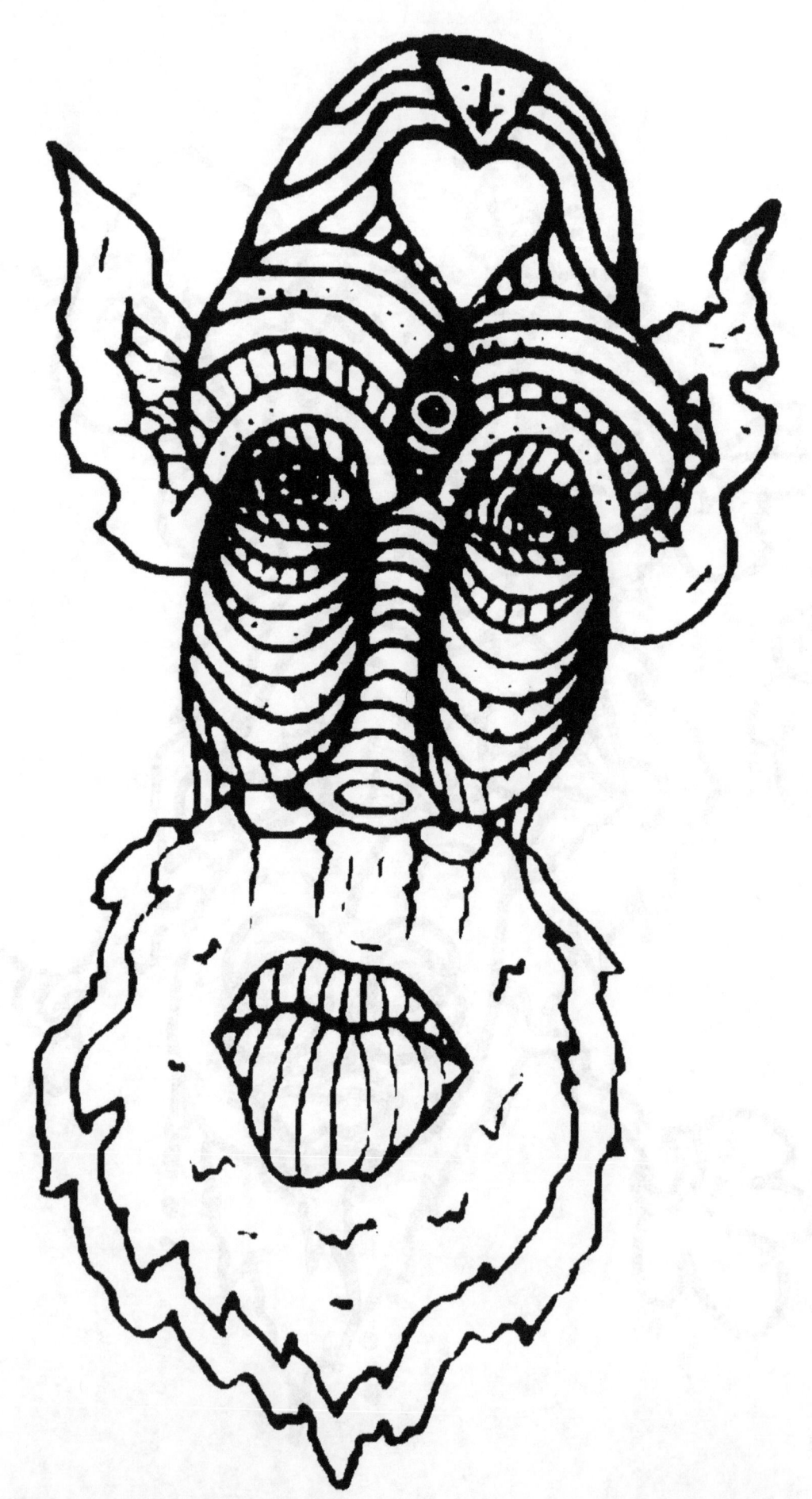

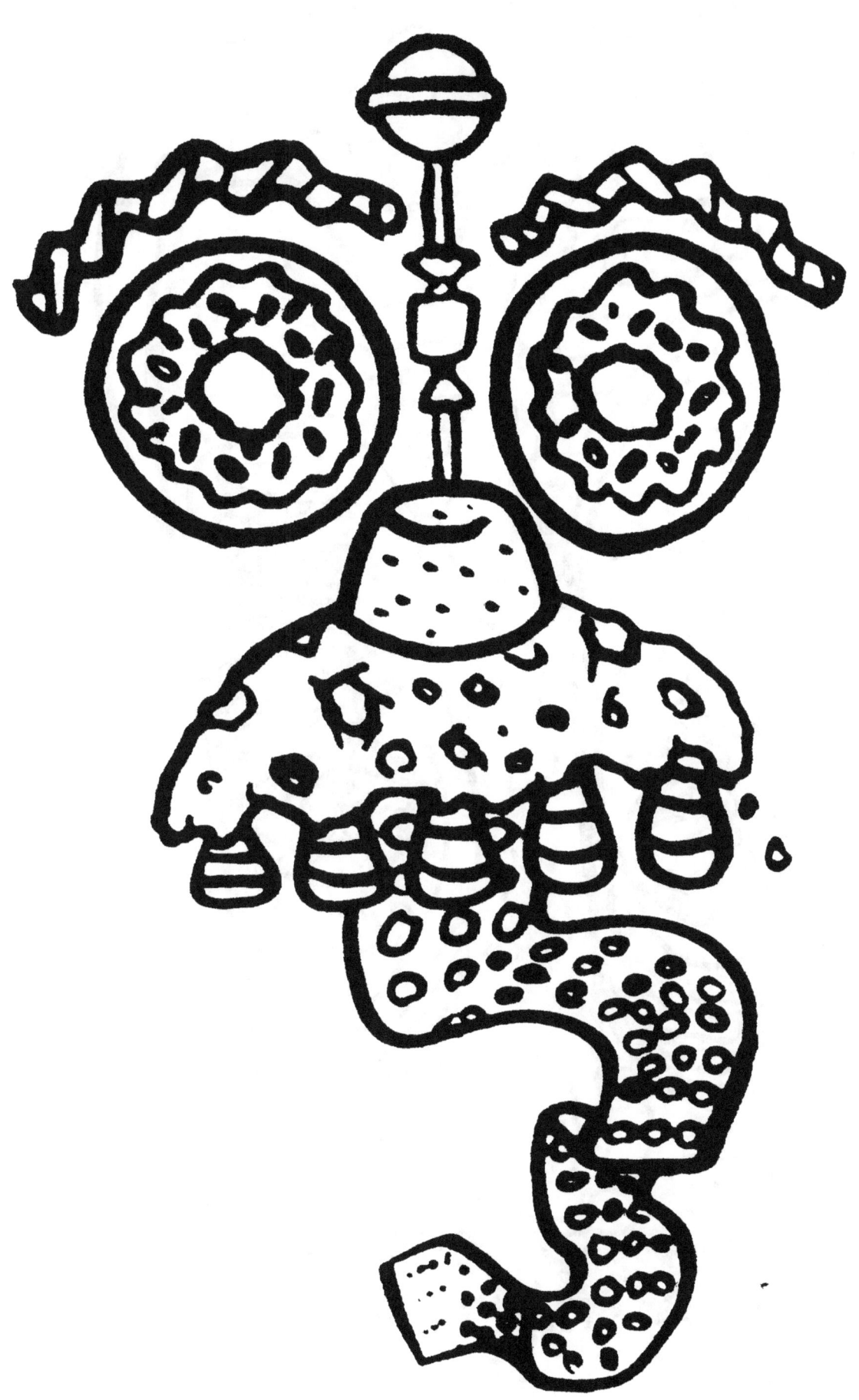

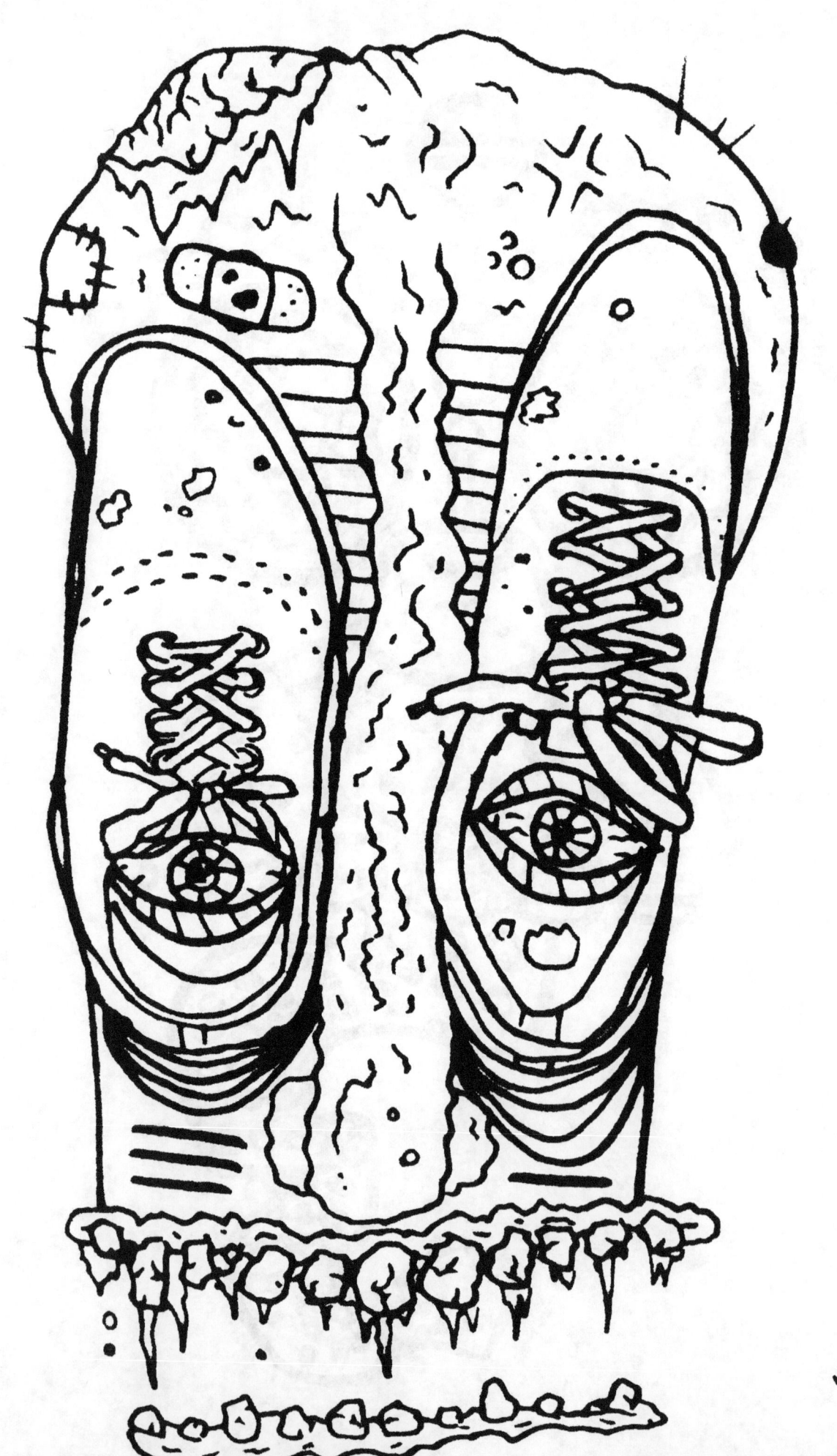

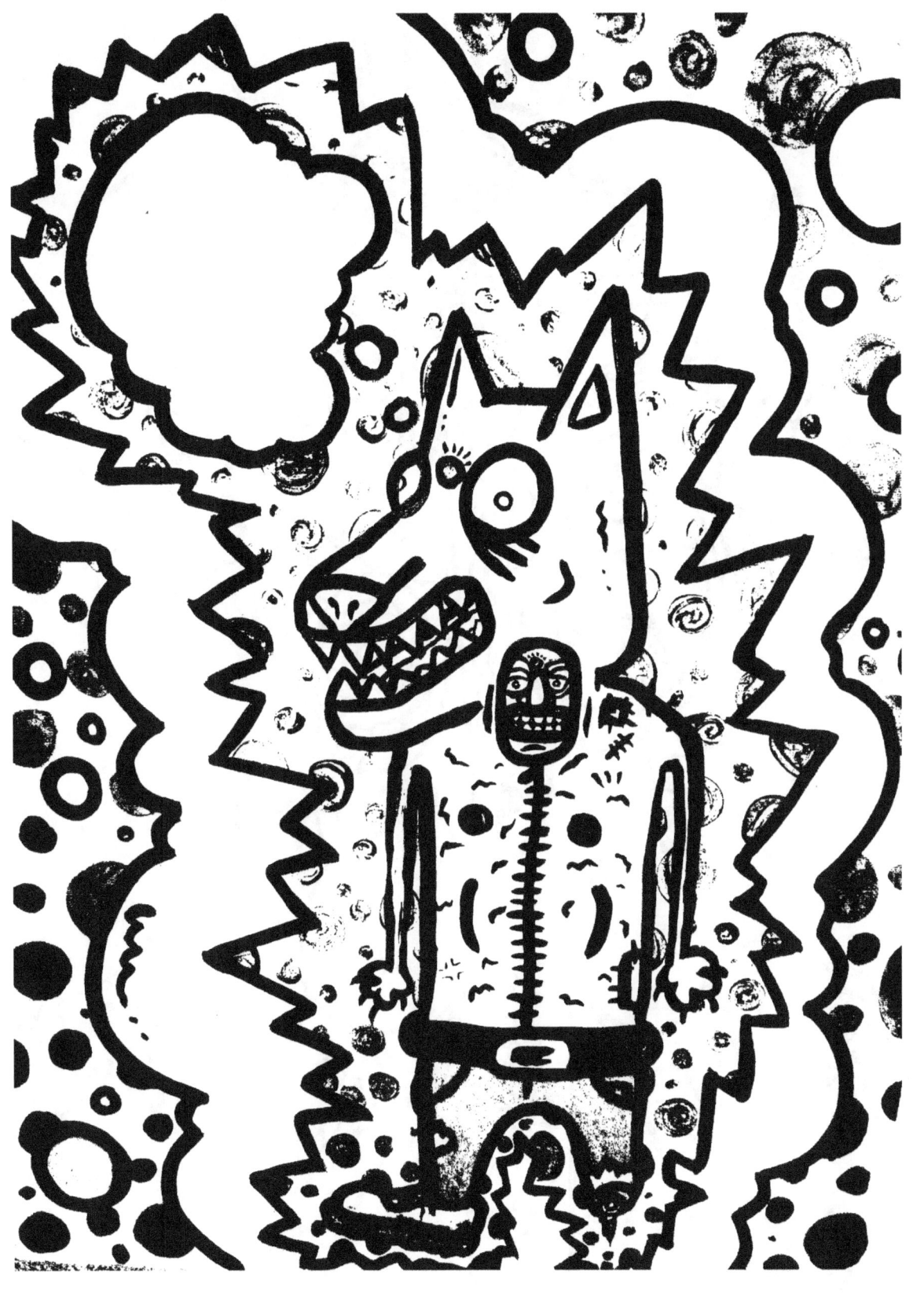

Fill in the empty thought cloud

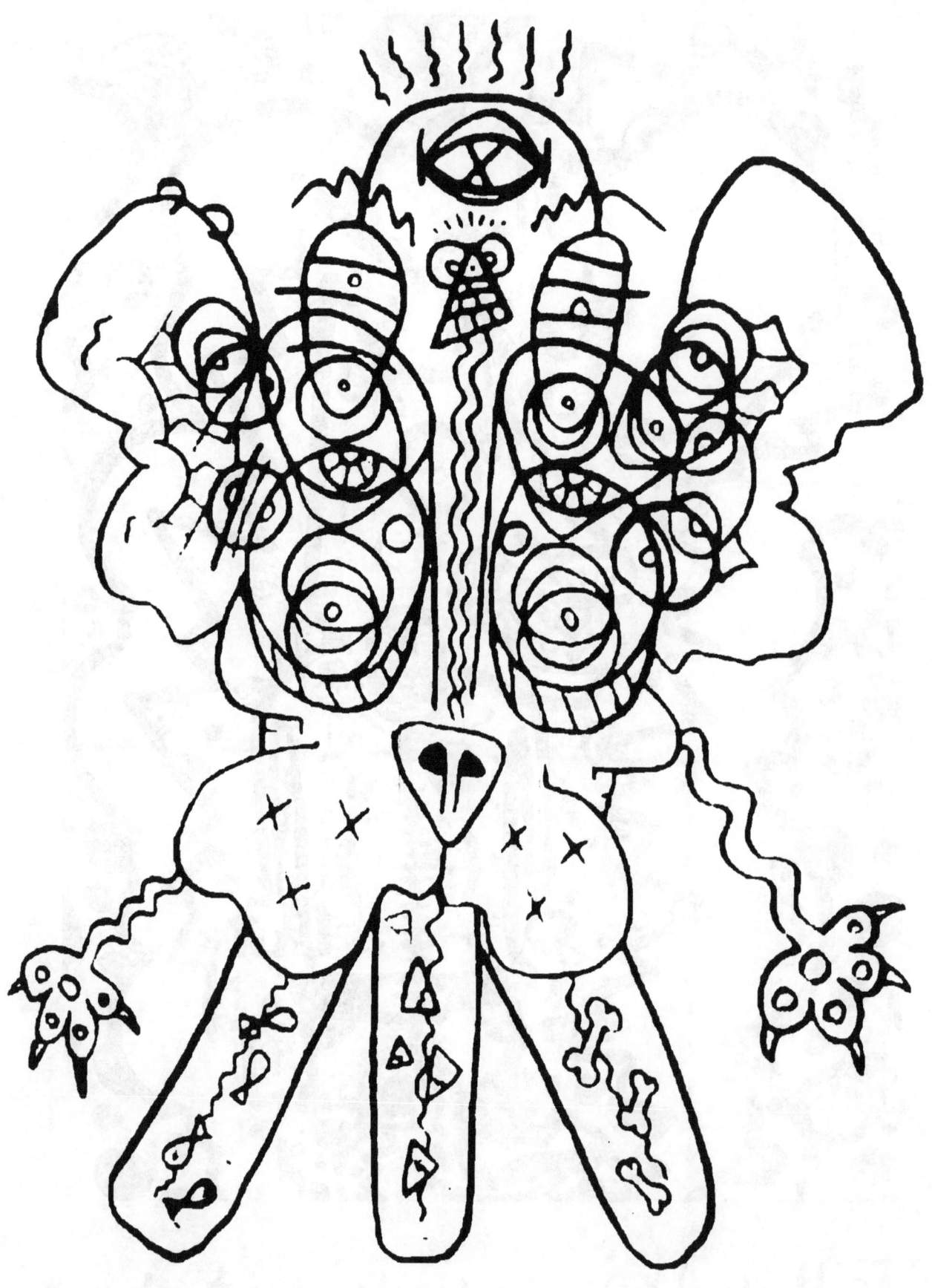

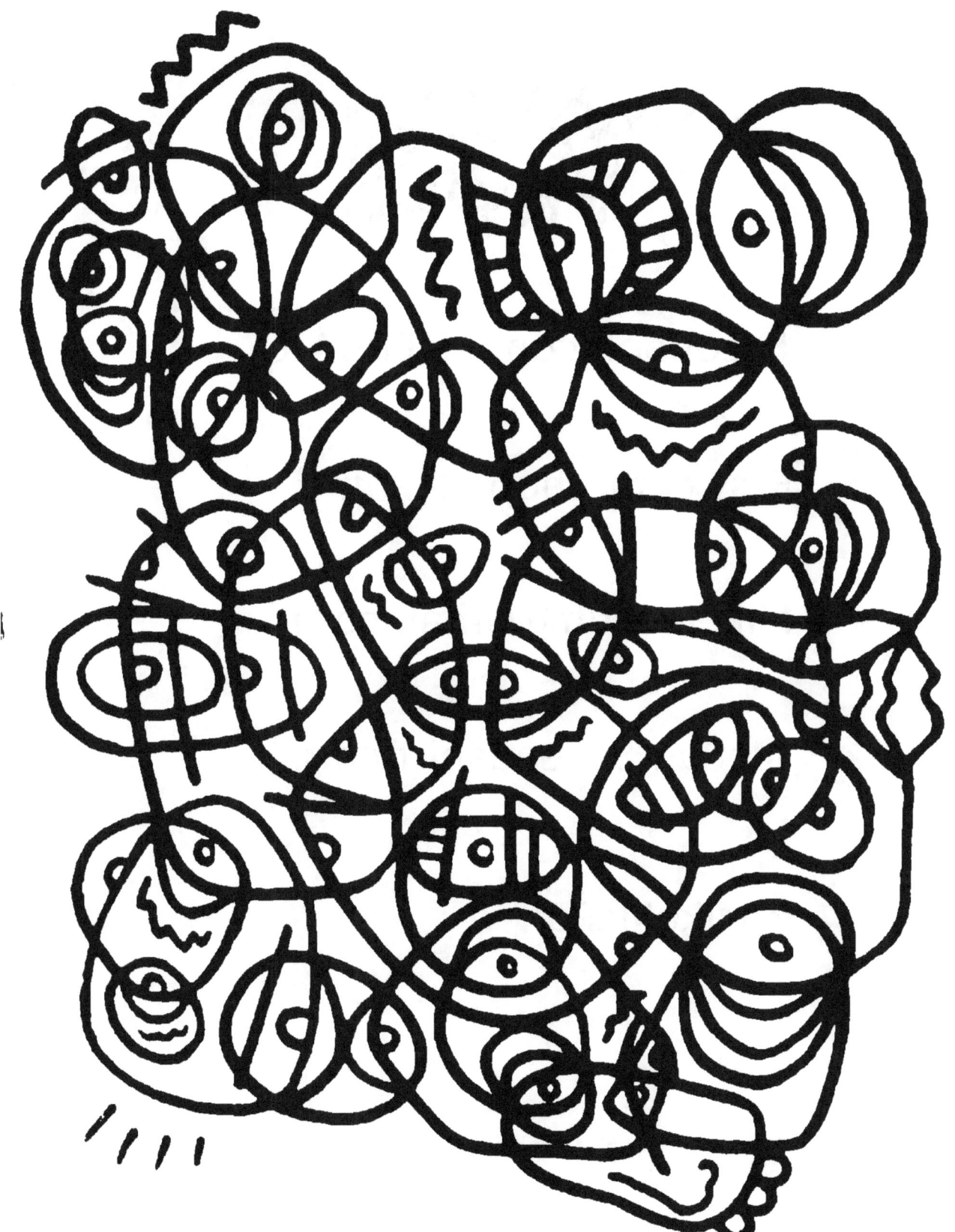

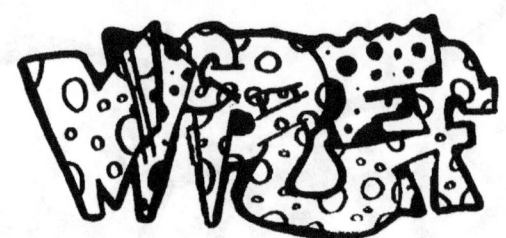

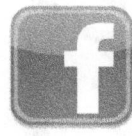 Facebook.com/McPuffArt

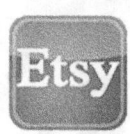 Etsy.com/Shop/McPuff

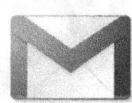 MikeMcPuff@Gmail.com

 McPuff.Spreadshirt.com

 @MikeMcPuff

www.ingramcontent.com/pod-product-compliance
Lightning Source LLC
Chambersburg PA
CBHW080632180526
45168CB00007B/3137